Beyond The Marketing Funnel

Playing Digital Mouse Trap To 10X Your Business

By
Mick Olinik

MickOlinik.com

INTRODUCTION

As a serial entrepreneur of over 20 years, I'm an online marketing strategist who's passionate about helping business owners and entrepreneurs start, grow, and thrive in their businesses.

There are several reasons I wrote *Beyond The Marketing Funnel*, but the most important is that while there are plenty of books about online marketing, email marketing, and funnel building, I've oddly never seen one that discusses *implementing a comprehensive marketing automation system for your business*.

Business owners and entrepreneurs need, and frankly, *deserve this knowledge* at their fingertips; and I believe this book does a good job of doing that in a way that's easy to understand and implement.

Table of Contents

Legal and Copyright

MickOlinik.com
109 S. Union Street, Suite 401
Traverse City, MI 49684
mick@rockstarcoding.com
www.rockstarcoding.com

Ordering Information:

Quantity sales. Special discounts are available on quantity purchases by corporations, associations, and others. For details, contact the publisher at the address above.

Printed in the United States of America

First Edition

Chapter 1. Child's Play

"By playing games, you can artificially speed up your learning curve to develop the right kind of thought processes." - Nate Silver

As a young boy growing up in Metro Detroit in the 1980's, my mom used to drive my brothers and me across town to go see our grandparents on a pretty regular basis. My grandparents were lovely people, but they lived in a community that was designed for older folks... not necessarily a nursing home, but you had to be over 55 to live there, and it was understood that everyone was supposed to be quiet. Since my brothers and I were in that mischievous age range between 7 and 12, we were naturally a bit frustrated as there was really no place for us to just run around and get busy with the business of being little boys.

Bless their hearts, for the amount of time that we spent at their home, my grandparents didn't really keep a lot of toys for us on hand either. What they did have was kept in the closet of a small room in the back of their condo. There was a Raggedy Ann doll (that lived up to her name, and didn't really appeal to any of us little boys), a large metal Tonka truck, a small assortment of puzzles with floral patterns on them, and a handful of board games.

One of those games was really cool. It was called Mouse Trap.

Dominoes, Mouse Trap, & Chain Reactions

Mouse Trap is a board game that was originally released by Milton Bradley, and it was basically all about setting up cool chain reactions, similar to the age-old game of dominoes.

If you've never played dominoes before or need a refresher, the easiest way to play is to line them up on their side sequentially in different patterns. You can set them up in a straight line, run them around the room, back and forth, or in any pattern or shape you want. The only rule is that each domino needs to strike another domino with enough force to knock it over when you push it in the right direction.

Once you have everything set up just right, you should be able to tip the first domino over so that it sets off a chain reaction that'll knock all of the other dominoes down in a one big giant chain reaction. It takes a lot of time to set it up, but it can be a thrill to watch it happen.

Mouse Trap is a game that's similar to dominoes, but instead of using uniform rectangular wooden blocks, Mouse Trap employs cool little toys that serve the same purpose. For instance, a reaction in Mouse Trap might start with a small plastic boot attached to a pendulum that swings back and forth. When you manually set the pendulum set in motion, you'd start the chain reaction inside of Mouse Trap, and the fun would ensue… it might look something like this:

1. First, the boot would swing forward and

2. Strike a small plastic bucket containing a marble. The bucket would tip over upon being struck by the boot, and

3. The marble would roll out and onto a predetermined track leading to your choice of several other obstacles. My favorite obstacle was a small plastic bathtub that was set up so that

4. The marble actually dropped off the track and landed inside of it. Once inside the bathtub,

5. The marble would roll towards a small marble-sized hole and

6. Fall two or three inches until it landed on the raised end of a seesaw (also known as a teeter-totter). This would obviously push the seesaw down and

7. Launch into the air a small plastic figurine of a man that had been positioned on the lower end of the seesaw. If positioned just right, that figurine would fly through the air and

8. Land in a well placed plastic bucket, which would, in turn, cause something else to happen.

Let me just tell you, as a 10-year-old prepubescent boy, it was a ridiculously fun set these chain reactions up and watch them run. My brothers and I would gleefully spend hours and hours setting up the Mouse Trap board in different configurations to see if we could make the reaction work in obscure, creative ways. We were obsessed with the thrill of watching it all fall down, even though it only lasted a few brief moments.

Digital Mouse Trap

Decades later (and 20 years into an online marketing career), I can't help put notice the obvious similarities between the overall concept of marketing and that Mouse Trap game I loved so much. Fundamentally, marketing is all about strategically coordinating a series of specific materials and tactics to achieve a desired outcome. Like Mouse Trap or dominoes, we painstakingly set our pieces up so that when we push them into motion, the resulting chain reaction will align perfectly to cause us to achieve our goals.

We often spend days, weeks, or even months going through the process of evaluating our target audience, deciding what mediums will be most effective in reaching them, and then setting up our marketing campaigns. Let's consider some real life examples.

Let's say that you are a local home improvement store, and you want to target homeowners who are looking to accomplish weekend projects around their homes. If you took a very traditional route, you might choose to put together a weekly circular for inclusion in the local newspaper, because you know that homeowners in your area still look there to find out what deals are available before they venture out on a Saturday morning.

Perhaps you are an insurance firm, and you would like to sell term life insurance to seniors. In this instance, you may decide that the most effective way to get your message to them is via a direct mail piece. Therefore, you might purchase a mailing list of seniors in the geographic area you want to target and send them a postcard offering term life insurance.

What if you have a very specific market that you are trying to reach? For instance, let's say that you are a gym that specifically tailors their workouts to women of childbearing age and older who want to lose weight, get more fit, and generally feel better about themselves. In this example, a better approach might be to turn to Facebook by creating a custom audience of women in a specific geographic area between the ages of 25 and 60 who have an interest in weight loss. Set up a promotion that leads to a landing page making an offer, watch your metrics, and make adjustments as you see what works.

Even more simply, maybe we just want to make an offer to our current and past clients by sending them an email. In that instance (assuming that we have continued to email them with regularity), we could easily queue up our newsletter program and send out an email or two with an offer.

Whoever you are and whatever your preferred medium tends to be, it's been my experience in working with hundreds of clients that these campaigns are typically very linear.

We decide what we are going to sell, come up with a concept for the promotional campaign, execute it, and then evaluate it once it's over.

In this way, the process is very cause and effect - action, and reaction.

It has a start, and it has an end.

And just as in the game of Mouse Trap, we need to set the promotion back up again piece by piece. In Mouse Trap, we had to set the obstacles up just right so that the marble ran down the track to cause just the right chain reaction. With our marketing campaigns, we had to define our products, come up with our campaigns, execute and evaluate them. It's the same thing - it has a start, and it has an end.

So then, what if I told you that it was possible to create a game of *digital* Mouse Trap that, if effectively set up and adjusted correctly, would just keep on running? That, if set up and adjusted correctly, the marble never stopped? Instead that marble would just keep rolling and rolling, continually tripping new triggers and perpetually creating that chain reaction.

What if I told you there was a way to replicate this with your digital marketing so that your prospects move through your sales pipeline in a very perpetual way? In a way that wasn't linear so much as a cohesive system, intelligently pushing prospects in the proper direction based on their previous purchases within your project library?

Many business owners look at that kind of prospect as a pipe dream, but it's very much a reality... and in this book, I'm going to show you how to make it happen.

About This Book

Before we can dig into the process of creating these perpetual cycles, we'll first need to lay some groundwork by discussing the fundamental components of marketing.

Note - this is a book about marketing that inherently uses online processes as a canvass to paint on. Therefore, you'll typically find that I use the terms "marketing" and "online marketing" interchangeably, because they are identical in principle. The difference lays in where they are being executed.

This book is broken out into two main sections:

1. The fundamental pieces of online marketing, including the development of a modern product library and the components of a sole marketing funnel, and

2. Moving beyond the marketing funnel, and learning how to morph a singular process into a cyclical process

The Fundamental Components of Online Marketing

In the first portion of this book, we'll cover lead intake (or lead inflow, depending on your industry or vernacular). Lead intake is exactly what it sounds like - the concept of acquiring, cataloging, and following up with leads.

We'll discuss the importance of indoctrination, which is the concept of introducing your target market into your ethos so that they drink your proverbial Kool-Aid and know, like, and trust you.

We'll also talk about what a modern product library looks like, and discuss the ladder of ascension - a foundational, lynchpin concept that is required to make just about everything I discuss in this book work correctly.

Finally, we'll dive into the actual nuts-and-bolts components that make up an individual marketing funnel.

Beyond The Marketing Funnel

The second half of this book is really about moving beyond the marketing funnel, pulling back the curtain and starting to see how we can look through the Matrix.

Instead of viewing your sales promotions as individual linear steps, we'll investigate where the linkage points are between individual processes that enable us to build circular flows so there's actual logic and intelligent, automated decision making.

So with that said, get yourself a pen and a notebook, turn off your laptop, silence your phone, and dig in. We're going to get deep into really what each one of these components really are, and then figure out how to make this work specifically for ***your*** business. Sound good?

Let's do it.

Chapter 2. Lead Intake

"I beg you to take a shot. Roll up on that hot chick in the bar and ask her out. Roll up on that good looking dude and ask him for coffee. Roll up on your business idea and make it happen. Because being 50, 60, 70, 80, or 90 and having regrets that you didn't swing the bat is the worst of them all. Our "at-bat" is in front of us - TAKE A SWING." - Gary Vaynerchuk

If you follow marketing blogs or podcasts, chances are pretty high that you are at least familiar with Gary Vaynerchuk. After graduating from college in 1999, Gary was given the day-to-day responsibilities of running his father's wine store. Shortly thereafter, he opened up online sales with the store, and in 2006 launched a daily webcast called Wine Library TV.

Being the huge, animated personality that he naturally is, Gary turned Wine Library TV into a smashing success. Over time, he leveraged his skills, fame and success and built one of the most prestigious social media marketing firms in the world - VaynerMedia. Known for his massive personality and no BS attitude, he's a genuinely sought after speaker. I won't lie - I'm a big Gary Vaynerchuk fan, and most people that I come in contact with seem to be as well.

In his talks and his books, Gary often comes back to a baseball analogy - "at bats". In case you are not a sports fan, an "at bat" in baseball is slang for a single opportunity to walk up to the plate, face the pitcher and either try to get a hit and get on base, or be put out. In a typical baseball game, most starting players will get 3 to 4 "at bats". The more "at bats" you have, the more opportunities you have to get on base, score some runs, and ultimately win the game.

Gary's assertion is that, as a business owner, you want to give yourself as many "at bats" as possible, and his analogy makes sense. Fundamentally, the more sales opportunities we create for ourselves, the higher our probability of success. After all, as long as our product is good, fills a need in the market, and is generally desired by our audience, our success is dictated strictly by the number of people who see our offer and are compelled to act upon it. The more opportunities you give your audience to see your offers, the more often they will be acted upon.

Understanding Lead Magnets

In online marketing, one of the best ways to get yourself an initial "at bat" with a prospective client is by using a lead magnet.

A lead magnet is mechanism we use to get people interested enough to connect with us and give us a little bit of information about themselves so that we can start a conversation. If we thought about fishing, a lead magnet would be akin to the bait that we put at the end of our hook.

Customer Relationship Management System

Lead magnets are only useful if you have a system available to collect and index those leads, and then actively do something with them. For the purposes of this book, I'm going to assert that the type of system that we are describing also has the ability to communicate with those leads, sell them things, and provide access to digital products in a systematic way that we can program. This type of system is often called a Customer Relationship Management system, or a CRM. It's called this because it inherently manages the relationships you as a firm have with each of your customers.

Almost all of the processes that we discuss in this book happen within the constructs of a CRM, or as an extension of a CRM, including the automated processes we use to market and sell different products to our customers. To that end, you'll find that we use the terms "CRM", "Customer Relationship Management software", "Marketing Automation Software", or "the system" interchangeably within this book.

Online Lead Magnets

There are a lot of different types of lead magnets, but for my purposes I'll divide them into two categories - online lead magnets, and offline lead magnets.

Online lead magnets are exactly what they sound like... lead magnets that are delivered in a digital format through the Internet which provide prospects with value in exchange for their contact information and permission to connect with them on specific topics. Typically we request a first name and an email address as contact information, but additional contact information like last name, cell phone number (for text messaging), and a variety of other types can be requested as well. The rule of thumb is that the more information you request in exchange for the lead magnet, the less likely your prospects will be to give it to you at all, resulting in a lower conversion percentage on your opt-in. For this reason, you want to choose what you are asking for carefully, and make sure additional fields are worth the slightly lower conversion rate.

Common types of online lead magnets include:

- E-books
- Video Series
- Interview Transcripts
- Audio Files

Let's briefly talk about each of these.

E-books are very common lead magnets, and are typically PDFs with some valuable tips or tricks that a prospective buyer may be interested in or find helpful. Further, it's been found that lists tend to perform well with this type of lead magnet. For example, new parents might be interested in a two or three page e-book called *The 7 Fastest Ways to Soothe a Screaming Newborn*, and further that this lead magnet would probably convert better than a longer e-book titled *Understanding the Psychology of the Screaming Newborn*. While both are certainly of interest to a new parent, the first may perform better, and it sounds much easier to quickly consume.

A free video series is another type of lead magnet that has recently gained massive popularity. As an example, an avid fly fisherman might be enticed to opt-in for a three video series describing how to significantly increase your chances of landing that really big fish using secret casting techniques that are best described visually.

Transcripts are also popular as lead magnets. Let's say do an exclusive interview with a famous celebrity, and you are interested in tapping into her fans. You could post pieces of the interview online, but offer the full, unedited version of the transcript as an effective lead magnet.

Similarly, audio files can be useful as lead magnets as well. For example, I could easily take an audio copy of this chapter of this book and offer it it as a wnloadable mp3... it's a great piece to use as a lead magnet.

Webinars & Facebook Live

Keeping in mind that the purpose of lead magnets is to capture contact information and permission to create a conversation based on a specific topic, we can actually expand our definition of a lead magnet to include additional prospecting activities where we are not providing a tangible product, but still creating significant value. Webinars are a great example of this.

With a webinar, you create the opportunity for people to consume your presentation in either a live or an evergreen format. In either instance, viewers preregister for the webinar so that you have a record of who is consuming the content. This also enables you to follow up with them via email (or text message if you choose). Webinars can be done live or "evergreen", which is effectively pre recorded and thus, on-demand. Further, evergreen webinars *can* be made to appear as though they are happening live, if creating that appearance is something that is important to you.

While webinars have been around for years, Facebook Live is one of the newer mediums being successfully leveraged to engage new prospects. Unless you religiously shy away from social media, I'm sure you are familiar with Facebook Live as it's quite prevalent and easy to do right from your computer, tablet or phone. With that said, if you master the art of Facebook Live and are able to effectively gain exposure, you can perform an audience grab, which is tactic commonly used by speakers on stage at conferences. The idea here is that during your Facebook Live (and while you have solid engagement), you can make a free offer of one of your tangible online lead magnets such as an e-book or a video series. When the tech is setup correctly, you can ask your viewers to text a specific word to a specific number which will both deliver the lead magnet to the prospect and enter that prospect into your system. For instance, a fitness professional that was seeking to employ this strategy might ask his viewers to text the word STRETCH to (212) 555-1212 in exchange for a video series.

Affiliate Marketing As Lead Intake

Affiliate sales and marketing can also serve as a highly effective form of lead intake. Many clients that my firm and I tend to work with deal in information marketing, and find quite a bit of success in this fairly underutilized model.

The concept is that you create a high value information product delivered in a series of PDFs or videos, and then price it attractively on a venue like ClickBank. This allows other people to sell the product on your behalf in exchange for a cut of the sales. If you make the price of the product attractive enough and offer a high enough commission, it can gain quite a bit of momentum, and generate a lot of leads for you.

Let's say, for instance, you sell a $10 product on ClickBank and offer a 90% or even a 100% commission on the product. If the product is actually good, other people will inherently be incented to sell it for you, because all they have to do is make the offer to their mailing list and collect all (or almost all) of the proceeds. If competitively priced, that offer will sell at a reasonable clip. While you, as the product's creator, will see very little (if any) money on the front end of the sale, what you do get is a qualified customer who has already displayed that they are interested in purchasing products that you have to offer. If you then take that qualified lead and feed them directly into your system, you'll be able to systematically begin to sell them additional products which you'll be able to keep the full proceeds from. When executed correctly, this is an excellent mechanism to build your business.

Offline Lead Magnets

Now that we've discussed online lead magnets, let's explore the more traditional style of lead magnets… offline lead magnets.

Before we get too deep into offline lead magnets, let's again revisit our definition of a lead magnet. Earlier in this chapter, we defined a lead magnet as a mechanism we use to get people interested enough to connect with us and give us a little bit of information about themselves so that we can start to have a conversation. It's the second part of this definition that can make offline lead magnets a bit tricky - the collecting information portion.

To that end, let's examine the case of a business card and ask this question… is a business card a lead magnet in and of itself?

I'd argue that the answer is no. While a typical business card contains the basic information necessary for a prospect to contact you, there's inherently no call to action, and certainly no way to collect the information. After all, basic information like your name, position, your company, phone number and email address are certainly useful pieces of information to know, but they won't help you index anything about your prospect.

I'd make the (somewhat controversial) assertion that the only way to truly make any promotional piece a lead magnet is to create an opportunity for our prospect to give us information about themselves in a way that we can *easily, automatically* add into our CRM. Anything short of that creates a potential weak point in our system, and thus can't be reliably depended upon.

Text Messaging (or SMS)

So how do you turn offline promotional materials into effective lead magnets? A simple, versatile answer is text messaging (also referred to as SMS).

In keeping with our business card example, you could easily turn that business card into a lead magnet by using a strategy similar to what we employed with Facebook Live. For example, let's say you run a carpet cleaning business, and routinely spend time at networking events. Rather than hand out a traditional one-sided business card, you could easily utilize the second side of the card to include a call to action told your prospect to text the word CARPET to (555) 231-1111 for a brief report on the 3 most important things you should take into consideration before you hire a carpet cleaning company. If the offer is compelling enough and the prospect takes you up on your offer, you'll be able to add his name, email address and phone number into your CRM very quickly, as well as have a basic understanding of what he was interested in when he initially engaged with you. Just like that, you've taken an offline promotional piece and turned it into an effective lead magnet.

We can employ this same type of SMS strategy to turn offline promotional materials into effective lead magnets with almost any type of printed material you can think of, including:

- Flyers
- Handouts
- Banners
- Books

I think that this strategy is fairly self explanatory, so I won't go in depth on each one of these. With that said, I do want to briefly touch upon books.

Let's say that you are a physical therapist, and you are looking for a way to bring in new patients. In your physical therapy firm, you work with a variety of different types of patients and are able to largely group them into three categories:

1. Athletes rehabilitating sports injuries,
2. Middle aged adults working through chronic pain, and

3. Mature adults dealing with the physical effects of aging.

A simple, effective strategy you could employ would be to write a book that contained six to eight short chapters, each one addressing a specific area of therapy in which your firm happens to be particularly well versed. At the end of each of these chapters, you offer the ability to download some additional information, most likely by texting in a specific word to a specific phone number and guiding the prospect through a few simple subsequent steps.

When this is done correctly, you'll end up with a multifaceted lead magnet that will also double as an awesome indoctrination tool (which we'll talk about more in the next chapter). Based on what a prospective client chooses to download (or not), we'll be able to identify exactly what type of client he or she might be. We will understand their problems and interests, and be able to better serve them by following up with information pertinent to their issues. Most importantly to the physical therapist, we'll be able to craft a systemic approach to closing more business so that they can help more people as well as become more profitable.

Audience Grabs From Stage

Finally, one of the most commonly used tactics involving SMS is doing an audience grab while speaking from a stage. We've already covered this when we talked about Facebook Live, but performing an audience grab while on stage is often far more effective, because you are working with a captive audience. If your talk is engaging, you can easily convert 80% to 90% of an audience by simply offering the slides from your presentation.

Real Life Example: Lead Magnets

Now let's look at a real life example. Last year, one of my clients in the nutrition industry put together a three day online summit. She gave the summit away for free, asking only for attendees to provide her with their contact information.

By running Facebook ads to an opt-in for a webinar, she was able to effectively promote and populate the summit. While she did presell videos of the summit prior to its opening as well as its recorded content after its close, the sole purpose of the summit was to create authority, goodwill and reciprocity amongst her attendees so that she could sell them a high ticket coaching program roughly a month later.

In this way, my agency was able to help my client use a combination of webinars to to funnel roughly 500 fresh contacts into her free online summit. A month later, we marketed her $1,500 coaching product to these attendees, which she converted at a rate of of about 16%, grossing her roughly $120,000.

Not bad for a free event, eh?

Exercise: Lead Magnets

Time to start putting this all into practice for your business.

At the end of this (as well as every other) chapter of this book, I'm going to ask you to do a short exercise that's designed to flesh out specific information about your business. As we get deeper into the book, I'll give you actionable steps that you can use to make real progress in setting up the automation for your business. Be honest with yourself and do the work, and I promise you that you'll reap the rewards. If that sounds fair, let's give it a go!

First, let's start by making a few lists of all of the different tools that you are using in your business right now. Grab a piece of paper and a pen and write down write down the name of the CRM that you are currently using. The answer will likely be one of the following:

- Infusionsoft
- Ontraport
- Active Campaign
- Salesforce
- Marketo

If you don't currently have a CRM, are using a different one than I listed above, or just aren't sure what it is, that's okay! Just write down what you know about it, and make sure to come back to it later if you need to research it more to find out.

Next, let's sort out what types of email marketing services you are using. Common services include:

- Aweber
- MailChimp
- Emma
- Constant Contact
- Sendy

You may be using something homegrown, and

that's fine too. Again, if you aren't positive of your answer, that's okay... but you'll want to find out as soon as you're able.

Next, I want you to create what may ultimately be a much longer list. Write down all of your specific websites, including any landing pages that you have. If you know what your websites are built with (WordPress is very common), then write that down next to each domain as well. If you are using a service to host your landing pages like LeadPages or Unbounce, write those down too.

Finally, create a list of all of your lead magnets. If you need help, flip back through the past few pages of this book to give yourself a refresher on what types of online and offline lead magnets are available, and see if you can't pair them up to the different ways that you are currently attracting prospects in your business.

Once you're done, let's move on to the next chapter.

Chapter 3. Indoctrination

"If people like you they'll listen to you, but if they trust you they'll do business with you." - Zig Ziglar

The mid 1980's saw the rise of popular celebrity Oprah Winfrey. Oprah's tabloid talk show, *The Oprah Winfrey Show*, became the highest rated show in the genre nationwide after just a few months, overtaking long-standing #1 talk show *Donahue*. The reason? Newsday's Les Payne observed, "Oprah Winfrey is sharper than Donahue, wittier, more genuine, and far better attuned to her audience, if not the world". In other words, it was Oprah's ability to build an immediate rapport with her audience that caused them to quickly trust and support her.

Several decades later, Oprah is now an international brand in and of herself. Following her long running talk show, Oprah launched the O Network, and is a philanthropist and a thought leader in the mainstream of American culture.

Similarly, the late 1990s introduced us to Peyton Manning, the all-everything quarterback from the University of Tennessee. The Tennessee Volunteers were extremely good with Manning at the helm, claiming a SEC Championship in 1997. Already popular with the public at large, Peyton continued on to the National Football League and was drafted by the Indianapolis Colts where he found significant success on the field, ultimately leading the Colts to a Super Bowl victory in 2006. Peyton's success and legendary on-field battles with rival quarterback Tom Brady of the New England Patriots gave him considerable opportunities to be in front of the public, which he successfully leveraged into his own celebrity persona outside of football. Even after his retirement from the game, Peyton continues to be a beloved public figure, and is paid well for his endorsements of products including Nationwide Insurance, Papa John's Pizza, and Omaha Steaks.

Peyton Manning and Oprah Winfrey are very different individuals travelling down very different career paths, but they share a commonality in the fact that through the opportunities that they've created to be in the public eye, they've garnered the awareness, affection, and ultimately, the trust of the masses.

Know, Like & Trust

Human beings are social creatures, and we're undeniably more connected to one another now than we have ever been in any point in history. Further, countless scandals and bailouts of entities "too big to fail" have contributed to the condition that the masses largely distrust faceless corporations. As human beings, we fundamentally want to do business with other people who we identify with, and who we view as experts in their field.

Put simply, **people want to do business with people that they know, like and trust**.

If we accept this premise, then our task as marketers is to reverse engineer the process of getting people to know, like, and trust us, and then replicate that for ourselves and our clients. Luckily, it's a fairly straightforward process... let me break it down for you.

Identifying Your Public Persona

The first step in putting together a successful indoctrination is to develop a clear idea of what your public persona should look like. *Your public persona is the sum total of your outward perception and communication to your market*. Everything that you say and do in public arenas (including social media) should serve to support that persona in a positive manner.

Next, with a firm understanding of the wants and needs of your target market, examine your background and selectively choose the core stories from your personal and business life that can be used to create a background narrative. We'll use this narrative as a basis for the "what" and "why" of your business, allowing us to create a connection and build rapport with your target market in a natural way. Our goal here is to craft a narrative that empathizes with our target market, create a sense of familiarity with them, and establish our authority with them so that they naturally trust us and what we have to say.

At this point, you may be thinking to yourself that this entire process sounds a bit fake and contrived, but I'd like to steer you away from that notion. To be clear, I would never making the suggestion that you fabricate stories or examples that did not actually take place. Instead, I'm suggesting that you package stories from your own history in a way that creates the narrative best suited to appeal to your audience.

Core Stories as a Canvas

Masterful storytelling is incredibly powerful, and by far the most effective method of getting a message across to an audience. The reason is fairly simple... being the social animals that we are, we love to listen to and engage in a good story. Whether we are at the movies, binge watching a series on Netflix, hanging out on Snapchat, or digging into a good old fashioned book, it's the concept of a story that always makes for the most engaging, consumable, and relevant content.

As marketers, the beautiful thing about stories is that they allow us to present concepts and ideas in a way that our audience will tend to both consume and readily accept. This differs from simply taking a specific position and making an assertion about a topic, as assertions have the tendency to invite opposing arguments. Therefore, because the purpose of indoctrination is to get our audience to know, like, and trust us, stories are our most effective tool. By embedding into them the core traits and philosophies that we want our audience to come to identify us by, we can effectively position ourselves exactly where we want to be while minimizing the opportunity for any objections from our would-be audience.

Indoctrination in Practice

Now that we've discussed indoctrination on a very strategic level, let's talk about the tactics of how we can actually use it in practice.

Indoctrination (or indoc, as I'll refer to it from time to time as shorthand), is a central ingredient in our online marketing recipe, and it needs to be initiated early on in the engagement of our prospect or brand new client. To this end, you'll look to begin the indoctrination routine whenever you have a new contact that comes into your ethos for the very first time, be that from any one of your lead magnets, or from one of your products that they have purchased.

From within your CRM, you'll want to set a rule that states that every new contact is automatically set to be entered into an indoctrination sequence as soon as the contact is created. A properly constructed indoctrination sequence typically begins one to three days after the contact is initially created within the system, and sends out a total of four to eight emails over the course of one to three weeks. Each of these emails should tell one of the core stories that you have identified about yourself, and should define one of the unique character traits or attributes that you want to make sure each one of your prospects understands about you. In this way, you can systematically create a consistent initial perception of your public persona, and have a strong foundation upon which to build your relationship with that prospect.

Keep in mind that this is an indoctrination sequence that will run concurrently with whatever the impetus was that brought them into your ethos, which is the reason that you don't begin the indoctrination sequence immediately. For instance, if they opted into one of your lead magnets for a free e-book, you'll obviously deliver that e-book immediately, and then follow up with the indoc sequence afterwards. If they purchased one of your products, you'll likewise begin the delivery of that product prior to beginning your indoc. In either instance, the initiation of the indoc sequence is automated and systematic, so that we know that our rapport building is happening in a consistent fashion.

When executed correctly, indoctrination is an incredibly useful tool to encourage retention and repeat sales because it provides a context for the lead magnet or product that the prospect or new client is consuming.

Real Life Example: Indoctrination

One of my clients is a leader in the health and fitness space who has successfully helped thousands upon thousands of entrepreneurs massively grow their businesses and change their lives. His personal story is inspirational and core values resonate with his audience when he's speaking on stage and in his sales letters, but he did not have a consistent way to get those stories across to new contacts before working with my team.

After setting up his marketing automation platform, he now has a cohesive, systematic mechanism to ensure that every new contact that finds their way into his ethos through any of his lead magnets, products, appearances, or books. This helps him set the stage to close even more business, and positively affect the lives of even more entrepreneurs.

Exercise: Indoctrination

Now let's focus on you and your business. Again, I'd like you to pull out your writing utensil and your pad of paper, and remove any distractions that may be nearby.

I'd like you to create a new list, this time of all the

features, attributes and traits that create your ideal public persona. What we are looking for here are the specific attributes that you would ideally want to convey to prospects and clients alike in both a business and personal context.

Once you've completed this list and feel good about its contents, think back to the business events that you have had the most success at while mingling with *new* people - these are typically networking events, business after-hours, or even individual sales and consulting appointments. Often, these are events that are not necessarily "salesy", but are more about relationship building.

If you are like most people, you likely have a handful or short stories or topics that you lean on to give people a flavor of who you are and what you do. What I want you to do is to write those stories down - not necessarily the whole thing, but just a couple of sentences so that you can easily identify them later.

Once you have the list of your commonly used stories, return to your list of the attributes and traits of your ideal public persona, and give some thought as to which stories specifically reinforce the idealized version of yourself that you want to present in your business. You may need to rework the way in which you tell some of the stories to highlight the traits you are seeking to convey, but so long as you remain honest in your storytelling, this will be an incredibly powerful way to introduce your prospects and new clients to who you are.

I cannot emphasize enough how important it is to spend the time with this exercise to get it right - trust me, you'll be glad you did. Once you feel good about what you've come up with, flip the page and I'll see you on the next chapter.

CHAPTER 4. DEVELOPING A MODERN PRODUCT LIBRARY

"When the product is right, you don't have to be a great marketer." - Lee Iacocca

The story of Apple Computers is one of the most compelling of the modern era. Playing the red-headed stepchild in the 1980s and 1990s, Apple was primarily a computer hardware and software company that had a difficult time competing in both primary sectors of its business.

On the software side of their business, Apple's operating system had a very difficult time competing with the predominant computer operations system of the time, Microsoft Windows.

Likewise, their hardware division (which only ran Apple's own operating system) was largely unable to compete with a bevy of hardware firms such as IBM, Dell, and Gateway that sold Microsoft-compatible hardware. However, massive changes were brewing in the consumer marketplace as the

90's were drawing to a close that helped Apple begin to stem the tide.

The late 90's saw massive upheaval in the way that media was delivered and ultimately consumed. File sharing services like Napster and Kazaa were rapidly reinventing the traditional media distribution channels, allowing the masses access to music and videos with an immediacy that was previously unimaginable.

Already gaining real traction in the personal computer market due to lingering public perceptions that Windows Computers were slow and virus prone, Apple was on the rise… and then they changed the game.

In January of 2001, Apple released their first official version of iTunes, their popular software for managing digital media files. October of the same year saw the initial release of the iPod, the walkman for the digital music world. The iPod set the world on fire, and Apple immediately became the de facto corporate king of digital media content.

The Modern Product Library

Today, Apple's collective product offerings have made them one of the most dominant companies in the world, transforming almost every facet of the consumer media market.

From a device perspective, Apple offers iPods, iPhones, iPads and their line of desktop and laptop computers, all of which come with free operating systems that are fully supported and have automatic updates.

From a software perspective, Apple offers suite of tools and utilities that are each specialized for use on their respective devices. They also run the App Store which is available on all devices, and features a simple and easy way for users to download programs of all sorts, from business productivity apps to games.

From a content perspective, iTunes is one of the leading outlets to purchase mp3s and movies. Additionally, Apple Music competes favorably with Spotify in the subscription-based music space.

Finally, from a utility hardware perspective, Apple offers just about anything else that a consumer or business might need to complete their digital existence, from wireless routers to the AppleTV to the Apple Pencil.

Apple's well developed product offerings epitomize what I refer to as the modern product library.

The modern product library is a collection of products that have been purposely designed to have two very specific, obvious characteristics: a natural ladder of ascension, and natural upsells.

Let's dig into both of these, and look at a few examples.

The Ladder of Ascension

The ladder of ascension is the concept of moving a prospect through a product consumption process where the cost barriers are initially very low and gradually become higher.

Initially, the prospect consumes a free or low priced product, has an extremely positive experience, and then looks for another product to consume that naturally builds upon their initial product. This next product is cross-sold within the initial product that has been purchased, and is available at a fundamentally higher price point than the initial product.

So long as the client continues to experience value and see results from the products that they are purchasing and consuming, it's inferred that there is a reasonable chance that they will purchase the next ascending product. In this way, a prospect that was initially only willing to provide a first name and email address in exchange for a free video series may ultimately purchase a high ticket coaching program that might be worth several thousand dollars a month.

From a nuts and bolts perspective, a simple example of a modern product library properly utilizing concepts ladder of ascension might have a have series of products that looked like this:

- Free Lead Magnet
- Low Barrier Offer
- Mid Range Offer
- High Price Offer

UPSELLS

Upsells are enhancements that can be added to a core product that increase it's usefulness or value. They're a crucial component to the modern product library because they can significantly increase the transactional and lifetime value of the product to which they correspond.

The classic example of an upsell can be found in a

question that we've all probably heard more than once in our lives - *"Do you want fries with that?"*

A side dish typically ordered along with an entree, french fries are a perfect example of an upsell. Rarely ordered alone, merely adding french fries to a burger can bump the transactional value of an entree at a burger joint by a significant percentage, while adding a drink as well can bump it even further.

Modern Product Libraries in Practice

Let's examine some real life examples of modern product libraries to help us illustrate what they look like and how they work.

We started this chapter off talking about Apple in detail, so let's break down their products a bit further. While there are admittedly a variety of ways to divide up their product library, Apple's portable content consumption devices *could* conceivably be broken down as follows:

- iPod (Low Barrier Offer)
- iPhone (Ascendant Low Barrier Offer)
- iPad (Mid Range Offer)

- Macbook (Ascendant Mid Range Offer)
- Macbook Air (High Price Offer)
- Macbook Pro (Premium Offer)

In this example, a consumer that was just being introduced to the Apple ecosystem might start with an iPod or an iPhone, their most attractive products from a pricing perspective. Upon having positive experiences with the initial product and being further indoctrinated into the Apple world, a percentage of the consumers who purchased the those low barrier products will ascend to a mid range offer in the form of an iPad or one of Apple's laptop offerings. Likewise, a percentage of consumers in one of those same mid range products will ascend to a higher priced or premium offer with one of Apple's higher end Macbooks.

If we look at the same product suite from an upsell perspective, we see an equally impressive list of options that are available to enhance the portable content consumption devices because Apple does such a great job of integrating its products. Upsells for any of the products listed above might include:

- AppleCare, which a warranty for any of the individual hardware products

- Downloadable Movies
- Downloadable Songs
- Software
- Wireless Keyboards
- Wireless Routers

While far from an exhaustive list, all of the upsells above dovetail into Apple's core product library perfectly, and significantly increase the lifetime value of their products.

Moving beyond Apple, let's take a look at several business models that more closely model your line of business.

HIIT Gym

Let's say that you are a fitness trainer, and you own HIIT gym (high intensity interval training). A simple way to structure your product library with this type of business model might be as follows:

- *Lead Magnet*
  Utilize a free three day trial to give prospects the ability to try out the gym at no risk.

- *Low Barrier Offer*
  Offer a low cost, 14 or 21 day fat loss challenge with a defined start and end date in which people can enroll. This allows them full access to unlimited classes in the gym for the entire duration of the challenge. The weight loss program also increases the chances that they'll see significant results, which they'll attribute to their experiences with the gym. This increases the chance that they will enroll as a full member. A sample rate for this challenge might be a one time fee of $49.

- *Mid Range Offer*
  Regular members pay one monthly fee in exchange for ongoing group coaching via unlimited classes at the gym. This such should be offered at a significantly higher rate than the fat loss challenge, and a sample rate for this membership might be $99 per month in this scenario.

- *Premium Offer*
  For members desiring additional attention, consider offering individualized one-on-one coaching at a premium rate. As this is type of service is not scalable, it's not necessarily a service that should be

encouraged. As such, pricing can be implemented to drive behavior, limiting the frequency that the option will be picked up as well as making it well worth it when a client does opt for it. In this instance, you would charge a premium fee that is congruent with how much your time is worth... perhaps $200 per hour or more.

Additionally, they are a variety of fairly obvious upsells that you could easily offer if you were a fitness trainer operating a HIIT gym, including items like protein powder, water bottles, and branded gym logo gear.

Info Product

Moving in a completely different direction, perhaps you are an information marketer with expertise as a nutritionist, and are looking for a way to monetize your knowledge. While there are literally dozens of different ways you could do so, a simple way to structure your product library with this type of a business model might be as follows:

- *Lead Magnet*
  Run Facebook Ads to an opt-in which provides a free video series containing some of your very best tips. This lead

magnet would serve to provide an entry point to your CRM, allowing you to automatically fire an indoctrination sequence as we discussed in chapter three, as well as initiate a marketing sequence for your low barrier offer.

- *Low Barrier Offer*
  Offer a 28 day email-based course that walks your client through your program day by day. Also include a private Facebook group for your clients to connect with you and your other clients. This promotes community, enhances client retention rates and creates a measure of accountability for your members. A sample price for this type of program might be a one time fee of $97.

- *Mid Range Offer*
  Available as its own standalone product or as an upsell off the low barrier offer, the identical 28 day email course could be coupled with both group and individual coaching, each of which would be remote. Group coaching would be made available at specific times during the month and conducted in a group video conferencing format. Further, participants would be offered the opportunity to schedule one

or two 20 minute video conferencing calls with their coach for individual coaching and direction. A sample price for this type of program might be a one time fee of $297.

- *Premium Offer*
  People interested in a more individualized experience could be offered a six week one-on-one coaching program for a significantly higher rate. This type of client would typically gain access to all of the nutritionist's other information products, and have regular calls with the nutritionist to gain both a personalized plan as well as accountability. A sample price for this type of program might be $1,000.

One of the great things about information marketing is the ease with which you can create upsells. As a nutritionist, there are the obvious physical products that could be offered such as supplements and shakes, but all information marketers can create an almost unlimited number of short digital products such as e-books, video courses and workbooks that can enhance the core product library.

Dry Cleaning

Finally, perhaps you are involved in a service-based

business model as a dry cleaner, and you are interested in expanding your core product library in an innovative way to better monetize your local market. In this example, a potential product suite could be designed as follows:

- *Low Barrier Offer*
  As dry cleaners will handle a shirt of a pair of pants for just a couple dollars, I'd make the argument that the typical standard service offered by most dry cleaners should suffice as a low barrier offer in and of itself. Typically any item between $3 and $5 each.

- *Mid Range Offer*
  For a monthly fee, the dry cleaner could provide an "unlimited" dry cleaning service by providing a reusable bag. The client would simply fill the bag up and bring it to the dry cleaner. Upon returning to pick up their dry cleaning, the bag would be returned as well so that it could be refilled and reused. A sample price point for this type of service might be $45 per month.

- *Premium Offer*
  Building upon the "unlimited" dry cleaning service, a white glove concierge version of the service could be offered as well. In

this model, not only would the client have unlimited dry cleaning, but the dry cleaner would include a pickup and drop off service as well. In this way, the dry cleaner is able to deliver a complete done-for-you, door-to-door service for the premium client. A sample price point for this type of service might be $120 per month.

Again, the upsells for a dry cleaner are fairly obvious but serve to increase the average transaction value. These might include services such as starching, folding, or emergency turnaround.

Real Life Example: Modern Product Library

One of my clients is an expert in helping women over the age of forty stay fit, live better lives, and deal with the negative physical and emotional effects of menopause. She had been an information marketer for years before she connected with my team and I, and as such had dozens of information products and memberships spread out in different places, being marketed to different lists of people with no real cross selling strategy.

After just a few months, my team and I were able

to successfully reorganize her existing products into a much more cohesive product library with a compelling ladder of ascension. She often likes to say that our team helped her transform her "promotion" business into a real, salable business with reliable, predictable income.

Exercise: Modern Product Library

Using the information and examples that we just discussed, let's get back to focusing on your business. Pull your pad of paper and pen back out, and again minimize any distractions that you have nearby.

Go ahead and create a new list, this time of every service that your business offers. If you already have a well-defined product library, that's excellent and this task should be fairly easy for you. If not, don't sweat it - just brainstorm the list.

After you complete your list, carefully review what you've written down and circle the products or services that you would consider to be core products within your business, rather than upsells.

Now, just looking at your circled products, reexamine them and decide what you think might be your low barrier offer. Place a "1" next to that product or service. In the same way, look for your next ascendant offer and place a "2" next to that. Continue this process until you have a number next to each of core products that you have identified.

Once you've completed this process, create two new lists - one for "Core Products", and the other for "Upsells".

Under "Core Products", write down the products you circled in the numerical order that you assigned to them from the lowest number to the highest number. This is your core product library in the correct order of ascension.

Write all of the products that you did not circle down in your "Upsells" list. These products are extremely important, and will help you increase the transactional value of your core products when they are leveraged correctly.

A Quick Note:

Don't worry if you find yourself having difficulty creating and organizing your list of core products for your product library - it happens to a lot of people! If you find yourself in this situation, consider asking yourself some of these questions which might help break you out of your mental logjam:

- Are there some services that I could offer a more abbreviated version of to create a low barrier offer?
- Is there a way that I could enhance my service to provide additional value at a higher price point?
- If my product is transactional in nature, is there a way that I might be able to repackage it into a membership or continuity based product?
- Is there anything that I could do to make my product or service a completely done-for-you, door-to-door experience for my customer?

The point of this exercise is to identify all of your products and services. In the same way that you might pull all of the puzzle pieces out of the box when putting a puzzle together, we'll want to be able to accurately identify our products and services properly and plug them into the right places in our automation systems later on in the book.

Once you feel you have a good handle on the product library within your own business, flip the page and let's keep rolling!

Chapter 5. Anatomy Of A Marketing Funnel

"We spend all of our time making money, so we can afford enough money to buy back some of our time." - Mick Olinik

With so many worthwhile things that we can spend our time and energy on in this life, I genuinely find the enormous percentage of the waking hours that most professionals spend working, thinking and talking about business to be remarkable - and I, myself, am no different. That said, what may even be more remarkable is how *many* of the talented professionals I talk to and work with claim that they despise sales and marketing, and either hate that portion of their job or are grateful that it isn't a portion of their job.

The core reason that so many professionals feel negatively about engaging in sales and marketing within their businesses is due to the fact that it centers around money. Because there are so many personal, familial, and societal pressures concerning money, it's fairly common to have psychological blocks around it as a concept.

Sales and marketing is nothing more than the collection of systems, processes, and verbiage that we use to entice other people to do what we want them to do. It's a way to manipulate situations to increase the likelihood of ending with the result that we'd prefer to create. In business, the only real difference is that we are attaching a financial value to the successful result.

If we look at it in these terms, we can demystify sales and marketing pretty easily. After all, influencing and manipulating situations is arguably a core, ingrained human instinct that we require for survival. For instance, babies that need to be fed or have their diapers changed cry at the top of their lungs until they receive the attention that they need. This crying is not a learned behavior, but is something with which we're innately born.

As we get we get a bit older and move into toddlerhood, we learn to control our attempts at influence and manipulation through trial and error. If you've ever been a parent to a toddler, you'll know that while the "terrible two's" are a real phenomenon, they are the direct result of the toddler learning to test his boundaries to see what actions he can take to elicit the results that he's looking to achieve. Make no mistake - these early experiments in learning to influence and manipulate the surrounding environment comprise the foundational components of marketing, while the corresponding success rate illustrate the fundamental concept of the sale.

Marketing, Sales, & Dating

Perhaps my favorite sales and marketing analogy that just about anybody can relate to is that of dating and relationships, and it ties in very nicely with the ladder of ascension that we discussed in chapter four.

When we are looking to date somebody, we are effectively marketing ourselves as a product and looking to get "buy in" from the person we're interested in. Each set of actions that we take to endear ourselves to our prospective partner is a really a marketing sequence, and we make a sale when we successfully get the reaction we're looking for.

Let's look at the entirety of a relationship, from start to finish.

In the beginning, you may just be looking to start a conversation with somebody, and so you might make a friendly, witty comment to them and offer to buy them a drink. From the perspective of the ladder of ascension, we can equate this process with a lead magnet.

Assuming they take you up on your offer, your next step is to engage them in conversation and see if there is mutual interest in escalating the new connection in a low risk way, such as going out on a date and sharing a meal. Taken again from the perspective of the ladder of ascension, going out on a date and having dinner with someone is a low barrier offer.

Assuming that the date goes well, you may both decide to escalate and ascend things in a more continuous way by going out on a series of additional dates and developing an actual relationship as opposed to a one-time connection. Looking again from the perspective of the ladder of ascension, this type of continued relationship is clearly a mid-range offer.

Over time, maybe that relationship becomes much more serious and you both choose to ascend and escalate it again by doing any number of things: moving in together, getting married, or making whatever other type of commitment feels right to you both. Finally, the perspective of the ladder of ascension would see this escalation as a high price offer.

Looking at the entirely of a relationship through this lense, it's pretty easy to see how dating and moving through different levels of commitment directly correlate with marketing and successfully closing sales within a product library.

Ultimately, marketing and sales are all about exerting influence on a situation and doing what you can to influence a specific outcome, and it's something that we all do every day of our lives. Whether we are making decisions about what to wear to work so that we are perceived in a certain way, trying to decide what to watch on TV with our spouse, or making a point in a business meeting, marketing and sales can be found in every facet of our lives.

The Two Types of Marketing Funnels

The term "funnel" is one of the biggest buzzwords in the current business environment, and people seem to have a lot of different ideas as to what it means. From my experience, there are really two types of marketing funnels:

1. *Product Library Marketing Funnels*, and
2. *Individual Product Marketing Funnels*

The approach I've taken in this book is to start with overarching ideas and then drill down to the more specific nuts and bolts of each concept. To that end, so far we've gone to great lengths to describe how funnel processes work within product libraries.

Product Library Marketing Funnels

Product library marketing funnels describe how prospects should *ideally* move through the product library as a whole. The most successful of these funnels begin by casting big nets that score easy wins, with each successive sales process getting more and more specific.

As the funnel progresses, prospects tend to self-select in or out. While this has the effect of cutting down the quantity of prospects that successfully make it to mid range and high end offers, it also makes sure that they are the *right* prospects, increasing our conversion rates.

While low barriers offers are designed to entice as many people as possible into the funnel, prospects can typically enter at any point, and upsell or downsell themselves as they choose. In this way, Product Library Marketing Funnels are designed to be top-down, but do not necessarily need to be linear.

Individual Product Marketing Funnel

Individual product marketing funnels describe the marketing, sales, and delivery processes of a *specific* product.

While there are nuances to different types of individual product marketing funnels, they differ from Product Library Marketing Funnels in that they are always linear in nature. There is a defined beginning to the funnel as well as a defined ending. Further, there are always four specific components that every individual product marketing funnel is comprised of:

1. Marketing and Sales Nurture
2. Purchase
3. Onboarding
4. Delivery

Let's discuss each of these four components in detail.

Component 1: Marketing and Sales Nurture

The first part of the individual product marketing funnel is the marketing and sales nurture component. This comprises all of the interactions that we have with our prospect that attempts to influence them to take positive action on the service or product that we have to offer.

From a tactical perspective, this is typically a series of systemic touch points that we have with our prospect that build to making a buying decision. Typically, these touch points come in a combination of forms, including emails, text messages, phone calls, direct mail pieces, and social media connections.

Component 2: Purchase

The second part of the individual product marketing funnel is the purchase component. This is the pivotal point where our prospect makes the actual decision to become a client.

From a tactical perspective, we need to make sure that a number of things reliably take place here. This includes taking and recording successful payment, removing our client from our marketing and sales processes for the product, adding our client to onboarding and delivery processes for the product, and notifying pertinent team members to follow up with the new client as necessary.

Component 3: Onboarding

The third part of the individual product marketing funnel is the onboarding component. Onboarding is crucial because it focuses solely on the customer experience, and sets the positive tone for an ongoing relationship.

As marketers, we often focus so much time and effort on *acquiring* new clients that we fail to realize that it's just as important to focus on our new and existing clients' experience. To that end, our clients tend to be happiest when they know exactly what to expect from us as product or service providers, and feel reassured in their decision. Onboarding is our opportunity to do just that.

To illustrate this a bit more, let's take a look at how effective onboarding can manifest itself in different types of business models.

Let's say that you operate a yoga studio and have a new client who has purchased a 20-class punch card. In this example, an excellent onboarding procedure would include a complete tour of the facility so that the client knows where everything is. It would also include some friendly direction as to where to go to find out about the schedule for different types of yoga classes, and how to sign up for a specific class. For good measure, an email could also be dispatched to the new member with similar information for their safe keeping.

Alternately, perhaps you are selling a digital membership product. In this instance, a quality onboarding sequence might be a series of two emails spaced out over the first three days of the client's new membership. The emails could be very simple, reminding the client to whitelist the email address so that they receive any emails that are sent out having to do with the membership. They might also include a link to a private Facebook group setup in support of the product, ad well as the email address to contact with technical support questions.

Component 4: Delivery

Finally, the fourth part of the individual product marketing funnel is the delivery component. This is self explanatory, as it is systemically delivering the product or content in the reliable manner you previously described in your onboarding process.

One-Click Upsells

While we've already discussed upsells quite a bit, there is a special type of upsell specific to online individual product marketing funnels called one-click upsells.

Once a prospect has successfully made a purchase in an online individual product marketing funnel, you have the unique opportunity to offer them a one-click upsell on the thank you page for the initial product sale.

These upsells work like any other upsell with the exception that the client does not need to enter their payment information a second time in order to make the purchase. Because we have already successfully processed their credit card information and have it in our system, the client simply needs to click a button to automatically purchase an additional product in a second transaction.

Psychologically, we've already influenced our prospect to make a buying decision. It's in this pivotal moment when our prospect is making a buying decision that they are most likely to make a *larger* or *additional* buying decision, and that's why the one-click upsell is so valuable. One-click upsells are emotional, impulse purchases and leverage natural human nature to be effective.

Furthermore, one-click upsells have magnified power because they are stackable. The upsell is offered with an accept or decline button, each of which leads to a page with another one-click upsell on it. In this way, stringing several one-click upsells together on top of the initial product can significantly increase our average cart value and our average transaction value.

Putting It All Together

Now that we've dissected each component of an individual product marketing funnel, let's briefly run down how it would work in an online environment.

To begin, prospects would enter the funnel via a marketing nurture sequence, mostly likely comprised of a series of emails directing them to a sales page for the product.

Once a prospect reaches the sales page and successfully makes a purchase, they're added to a purchase sequence which triggers a variety of rules depending on the nature of the product. Typically, this will include removing the prospect from the marketing nurture sequence, and adding them to the onboarding and content delivery sequences associated with the product.

The thank you page that the new client is delivered to following their successful purchase contains a one-click upsell, which is an additional product that augments the product that they just purchased. The client can choose to either accept or decline the upsell, at which point an additional one-click upsell is displayed. Should the client click neither, no action will be taken and the only purchased that will be processed will be of the original product.

Two to three upsells are commonly added to online individual product marketing funnels.

Real Life Example: Individual Product Marketing Funnels

One of my clients is a medical doctor who specializes in weight loss via clean protein. By running YouTube and Facebook ads to video-based lead magnets on topics that include fighting inflammation and discovering how to *affordably* feed your family healthy food, she's able to mine a deep well of qualified prospects for her coaching programs and information marketing products.

Prospects who move through her video-based lead

magnets are then added into the marketing nurture sequence that is associated with her $297 coaching program. When people purchase her program, they are immediately offered a one-click upsell for a quickstart package containing a month's worth of nutritional supplements and protein shakes for an additional $147.

After a period of 10 days, prospects who choose not to purchase her $297 coaching program are instead offered a downsell to purchase her more affordable $97 program which mirrors the $297 program, sans the coaching. In this way, we are able to help her attack her market by using a mid-range offer with both an upsell and a downsell to both maximize her gross revenue as well as her overall conversion percentage.

Exercise: Individual Product Marketing Funnels

We've just gone through quite a bit of material, and now it's time to apply it to your business.

To help get you started, I've prepared some PDFs for you that you'll want to download.

Text the word FUNNEL to (231) 222-4118

Follow the instructions. You'll be prompted for your email address, and in just a few short moments you'll receive an email with a link to download two files.

The first file is a model of the individual product marketing funnel, completed in full for a sample product.

The second file is a duplicate of the first, with the exception that the boxes are blank and have plenty of space to write in.

Print both maps out, and then select one of your products and begin to fill the map out so that you can see exactly what this process might look like within your business. This process will really help you understand how the individual product marketing funnel works, and how it can help you systemize your business.

END OF PART ONE

Early on in this book, we mentioned that it was essentially written in two parts.

The first part of the book has addressed each of the fundamental pieces of online marketing, including lead intake, lead magnets, indoctrination, CRMs, product libraries, the ladder of ascension, and the fundamental types of funnels.

Now that we've covered these foundational concepts, I want to show you how to transform that linear model into a cohesive, powerful cyclical system that'll really help you 10X your business. If you are ready for it, let's jump into Part Two!

Chapter 6. Beyond The Marketing Funnel

"It's not the customer's job to know what they want."
- Steve Jobs

Being the marketing geek that I am, I often find myself interested in breaking down different marketing and sales strategies that I come across in daily life. One of my favorite strategies can be found by looking at the physical layout of warehouse stores like Costco.

Every Costco is fundamentally organized with a rectangular layout that's similar to a racetrack. As customers walk into the store, they are naturally steered towards the track, which features different departments with high profile shelves on the outer edges of the store, and low profile shelving allowing you to see different types of products in the middle of the store.

Staple items such as light bulbs, detergent and toilet paper are all spread out in different areas of the store. This forces shoppers to move through aisles in the store that they may not have otherwise.

By setting their stores up in this way, Costco can effectively gain a measure of control over the traffic flow through their stores.

Consider that any given aisle in a thoughtfully designed store such as Costco will typically contain a singular type of core product, as well as products that add additional value to the core product. For example, an aisle with pet food will often have additional pet products such as treats, kitty litter, and travel carriers.

When a customer in need of a staple product like toilet paper is forced to pass the pet food to get pick it up, Costco not only creates the opportunity for the customer to purchase pet food, but to additionally upsell themselves on other pet-associated items. This increases the number of impulse purchases the average customer makes.

As we noted earlier in the book, Gary Vaynerchuk refers to this concept as creating as many "at-bats" as possible. The more "at-bats", or opportunities, that you create to sell product, the higher your probability for more sales.

Costco's approach to store design systemically elevates their number of "at-bats" by naturally increasing their customers' exposure to both different categories of products as well as the raw number of products. Both of these factors act as effective multipliers to bottom line sales.

Aisles As Funnels

Individual aisles like you see in a well designed store such as Costco are the closest thing we have to a physical representation of an individual product marketing funnel. After all, if the core product in the aisle is pet food, we are naturally offered the opportunity to purchase related products such as pet treats and pet toys.

The brilliance of Costco's racetrack is that, through the clever design of the store's layout, Costco is able to manipulate their customers' movement in such a way that they actually expose them to all of their aisles. In other words, they are able to *physically* set up their product library marketing funnel so that they maximize the number of individual product marketing funnels that their customers are exposed to.

Costco is hardly the only store that utilizes these types of physical strategies to create opportunities for their customers to move through different aisles. Creative product placement, end caps and various sales promotions are used throughout the retail industry. Nonetheless, marketing and sales processes lacking the advantage of a physical, in-person component often find moving prospects through an individual product marketing funnel to be a manual, hand-to-hand process.

It doesn't have to be this way, though. By using some well defined (albeit mildly complex) marketing automation processes, you can actually tie multiple funnels together. In this way, you can take an individual product marketing funnel and transform it from a singular, linear process into a powerful, automated system.

The Marketing Conveyor Belt

In its most simple form, the marketing conveyor belt is an alternate way to organize your product library marketing funnel.

You may recall that product library marketing funnels are typically top-down processes. Low barrier offers are used to entice as many people as possible into the funnel, although prospects can enter at any point and upsell or downsell themselves as they choose.

Marketing conveyor belts work in a similar way, with

the exception that they provide a mechanism for an automated return to the top of the funnel once the prospect reaches the bottom. In this way, conveyor belts borrow a concept from Costco's racetrack in that they provide a natural mechanism to move contacts through different individual product marketing funnels, thus increasing our total number of "at-bats" and our bottom-line revenue.

Regardless of whether they initially opted into a lead magnet or purchased a specific product, conveyor belts give us quite a bit of flexibility over how our products are offered to both our prospects and clients. Through the magic of automation, we can not only make sure that each of our products are offered to each of our contacts who have not yet purchased them, but we also have tactile control over the timing and frequency of those offers, as well as what to do when our contacts don't take us up on them after repeated attempts.

Ultimately, a contact will interact with each product within the conveyor belt to reach one of three different results. For each product, the contact will either:

1) Purchase the product initially,

2) Initially decline the product, choosing instead to purchase the product later on

following additional rapport-building and indoctrination, or

3) Decline the product after it's been offered as many times and in as many ways as we've chosen to offer it.

Automating The Ladder Of Ascension

The beautiful thing about conveyor belts is that they provide an automated mechanism to assist our prospects and clients with the process of moving themselves up the ladder of ascension and through a product library.

Conceptually, when a prospect initially enters the system via a lead magnet, the first product that they are offered is the low barrier offer at the top of the product library marketing funnel. When that prospect converts on the low barrier offer and becomes a client, the conveyor belt moves through a standardized process to automatically begin offering them the next obvious product within the product library.

Should the prospect choose to not purchase a specific product, the conveyor belt provides the mechanism for that client to be reintroduced to the product at a later date when additional rapport-building and indoctrination has taken place. In this way, we provide ourselves with an additional "at-bat" to derive revenue from this product, with an increased chance to close since more time has passed and a better relationship has been built.

When executed correctly, a conveyor belt serves as the backbone of an automated, structured digital marketing and sales process that reliably creates predictable, loyal buyers.

Finally, it's crucial to note that a well developed conveyor belt should not be overly aggressive. Otherwise, you risk your contact self-selecting out of the program as a whole. The measure of what is or isn't considered overly aggressive is very subjective, and is entirely dependant upon the preferences of each business's target audience.

Selecting A Marketing Automation System

By definition, marketing conveyor belts need to be built on a singular web-based marketing automation framework. These frameworks serve as the chassis for the marketing automation systems that we create.

While there are new frameworks coming out all the time, the two of most prevalent frameworks for companies operating in the small to mid-sized enterprise space are Infusionsoft and Ontraport.

NOTE: While everything we'll discuss is conceptually the same, this book focuses on marketing automation solutions for small to medium sized companies, loosely defined as those with a revenues below $5,000,000 annually.

Infusionsoft

The most widely used of these two frameworks is Infusionsoft, and for several reasons. First of all, Infusionsoft predates just about every other marketing automation framework by about a decade, and as such has had a corner on the automation market during the adolescent stages of the Web.

Secondly, and more importantly, Infusionsoft excels for small and medium sized brick and mortar businesses and franchises who can benefit from automation in their sales processes which tend to be fairly long and complex. Consultive services such as custom home builders or financial planners can really take advantage of their advanced sales pipeline capabilities.

Infusionsoft is an extremely powerful system that can have its functionality extended via third party plugins and services that cater specifically to Infusionsoft clients. In this way, there are few capabilities that cannot be created *in some way* with Infusionsoft, but you may need to be creative in how you accomplish them.

ONTRAPORT

An all-in-one marketing automation system coupled with a robust CRM, Ontraport provides an impressive number of native features that are required in order to effectively create our funnels and conveyor belts.

Ontraport is particularly effective for businesses that largely operate online. For information marketers that sell digital products and group based remote support via communities, Ontraport is a uniquely powerful solution. The framework's ability to natively connect with and control an unlimited number WordPress based membership sites, as well as it's native one-click upsell capability makes it a no-brainer for web-based businesses.

As a professional who owns a marketing automation implementation agency, I can tell you from direct experience that the best solutions are found by minimizing the number of third party services required to make your marketing automations happen.

Fewer connections between crucial, mission-critical systems equate to fewer critical breakpoints in your marketing automation system. Further, it's always most ideal to house those processes directly within your CRM. For this reason, I almost always recommend either Ontraport or Infusionsoft to my clients, dependant upon which native systems are most appropriate for their specific business.

Other Marketing Automations Solutions

Although they are the most robust, Infusionsoft and Ontraport are certainly not the only products in the marketing automation space. Here are a few other notable services that are worth mentioning and considering for your business, dependant on your requirements and budget.

- *ConvertKit*
  An up and coming marketing automation platform, ConvertKit is notable because its focus is on acting as a no frills CRM with excellent marketing automation features. Because it places a significant emphasis on the ease of use of its API, ConvertKit integrates with a remarkable number of

services. It also boasts a comfortable price point.

- *ClickFunnels*
  ClickFunnels is not a marketing automation platform per se, but a landing page and funnel generator with robust onboard split testing. It's worth paying attention to because of its relative ease of setup and rapid adoption by a new wave of web-based entrepreneurs, as well as its corresponding CRM product which snaps directly into it.

- *Active Campaign*
  Sporting an easy-to-use visual campaign builder, Active Campaign does a nice job of providing the fundamental capabilities required for building simple to intermediate marketing funnels for an attractive price. Advanced users may become frustrated with its lack of precision control.

Components of a Conveyor Belt

Now let's take a look at the actual individual components that make up a well-developed conveyor belt, and how they fit together. While we several of these components are pieces that we are very familiar with and have already discussed in detail, others are new and specific to a conveyor belt's construction.

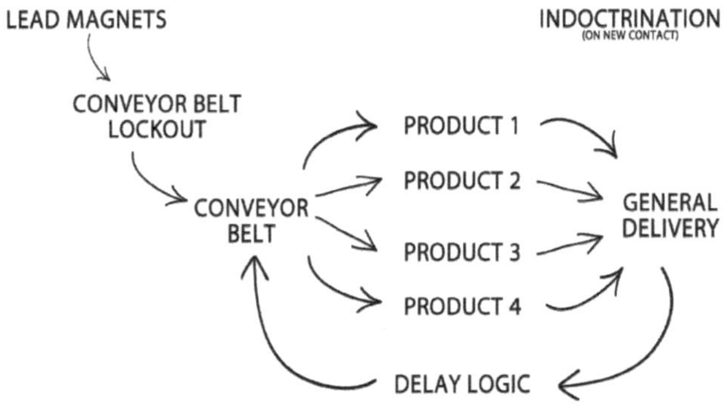

A simple version of a conveyor belt would typically include the following components:

1. A Collection of Lead Magnets
2. Indoctrination
3. A Conveyor Belt Lead Magnet Lockout
4. A Master Conveyor Belt Logic Board
5. Individual Product Marketing Funnels
6. Individual Product Delay Logic
7. General Delivery

The “new” pieces that we need to look at here include the lockout, master logic board, and delay logic. All of these govern the way in which the conveyor belt operates as a whole, and are essential to the process.

Here’s how a conveyor belt works in practice.

Lead Magnets & Indoctrination

When new contacts are initially introduced to you through any type of a lead magnet such as a webinar, e-book, or an SMS optin, two things take place immediately. First and most importantly, we follow through on that opt-in and deliver whatever content we promised. It’s crucial to deliver this information promptly and as expected, as it starts our relationship with the new contact in the right way.

Secondly, because the contact is brand new to our ethos, we automatically initiate an indoctrination sequence that’s designed to begin a day or two after the initial opt-in is made, automating the process of building rapport.

The Lockout & The Logic Board

Since the purpose of the conveyor belt is to intelligently automate the marketing of each product in your product library, we need a way to tell the system which product is appropriate to be marketed to any given contact next, based upon their previous actions within the system. This is what the conveyor belt logic board does, acting as the master authority to direct traffic throughout the system as a whole.

In order to make sure that we have tactile control over what marketing messages our prospects are receiving, we need to make sure that they are only entered into the conveyor belt once. This is why we use a conveyor belt lead magnet lockout to manage which contacts are permitted to into the conveyor belt logic board.

The way it works is quite simple. Depending on the nature of the lead magnet, it can take anywhere from just a few minutes to several weeks to deliver and fulfill completely. However long the timeframe, once a lead magnet has been completely delivered to a contact, that contact's information is fed into the lockout. If the contact has already been fed into the lockout and is in the system, then nothing else happens. If, however, the contact is brand new and has never been entered into the system, it passes through to the logic board.

The logic board orients our product library in accordance with our ladder of ascension, and directs our prospect to the correct individual product marketing funnel within that hierarchy based on whether or not they've already purchased it, or have chosen *not* to purchase it a specific number of times that we can define.

Individual Product Marketing Funnels

Since we've devoted the better portion of a chapter to individual product marketing funnels, we won't dwell on them here. Once a prospect has been pushed into a specific, individual marketing funnel, that funnel operates exactly as we would expect it to. This results in one of two outcomes - the prospect either:

1. Purchases the product (and any upsells being offered), and is entered into onboarding and delivery sequences, or

2. Does not purchase the product, and we record the fact that the product was offered and not purchased.

Regardless of the outcome, we then move our client to a delay sequence. However, before we can really understand the usefulness and importance of a delay sequence, we need to understand general delivery within a conveyor belt.

General Delivery

General delivery is the specific component in a conveyor belt that handles rapport building past initial indoctrination. For the most part, it's comprised of the emails that you send out to your list on a regular basis, but general delivery can include communication types other than just email, and it functions a bit differently than what most marketers are used to.

When most email marketers using conventional newsletter platforms mail out to their list, they do so by sending a broadcast. Those broadcasts are typically either sent as immediately, or they are scheduled to be sent out later.

Philosophically, emails being sent out in a conveyor belt are handled differently. Rather than sending out blanket emails to an entire list, communications are divided into two different types - general delivery emails, which are content-based, relationship-building communications, and individual product marketing emails, which are obviously communications designed to market a specific product. Broadcast emails are reserved for crucial times when it is absolutely necessary to communicate with everybody in your list, regardless of where they are in the sales and marketing process.

In a conveyor belt, we manage our general delivery communications in a specialized type of list housed in your marketing automation software called a date sequence. Date sequences are incredibly useful because they can be paused or unpaused on a subscriber by subscriber basis. This means that we can have individual contacts receiving a stream of rapport-building communications for a requisite amount of time before we *pause* those communications, replacing them with very specific marketing communications unique to their ascendant progress through our product library. Once that prospect has either purchased the product or chosen not to, we can *unpause* them in the general delivery sequence and resume our regular rapport-building activities with them.

What this means is that different contacts in a conveyor belt may or may not be receiving emails from a general delivery list, depending on whether or not they are actively engaged in an individual product marketing funnel.

By focusing on either rapport-building or an individual marketing funnel, we can focus our message, keep our unsubscribes down, and create an automated system to deliver marketing messages on all of our products in a way that is not overly aggressive.

Delay Sequences & Delay Logic

The final component of the conveyor belt is delay logic, which is housed in a delay sequence for a specific product.

As stated earlier, once a contact is moved into an individual product marketing funnel, they will either choose to purchase the product or not. Regardless of the outcome, the contact is then moved into a delay sequence.

A delay sequence is the vehicle that houses the logic which unpauses general delivery for the contact, as well as specifies the period of time that the contact will remain in general delivery before once again being paused and rerouted into the next individual product marketing funnel.

Since each product has its own delay sequence, each product can have its own set of delay logic, allowing for varying time differentials between specific products. Further, each product can theoretically route to its own set of related products, creating the opportunity to branch a product library while still keeping it within the conveyor belt as a whole.

In this way, delay sequences and the delay logic they contain create the glue that binds a conveyor belt together. They form the rules that govern which contacts are pushed into which individual product marketing funnels, and eventually push the contact back into the very top of the conveyor belt logic board itself, closing the loop and creating a perpetual process.

The Conveyor Belt in Practice

Now that we've gone through the theory of what a conveyor belt is and how it works, let's take look at a hypothetical example of how it actually functions in the real world, from start to finish.

Let's imagine that you are business consultant and have a variety of online based lead magnets. You have several e-books that prospects can opt in for, a free video tutorial series, and a hard copy book that you are offering in a free-plus-shipping offer (with requisite one-click upsells).

You are invited to speak at a conference where you perform an SMS-based audience grab, offering your slide deck in exchange for an audience member's contact information. The talk goes fabulously, and you get quite a few opt-ins for the slide deck - one of which is a gentleman named Joe Smith.

Joe has never heard of you before, but he's really impressed during your talk. Upon texting the word SLIDES to (555) 555-1212 as you directed during your speech, he gets an immediate text response back that says:

```
Hi there! I'm so glad you are interested in my slides! Go ahead and respond to this text with your first name and email address, and I'll send it to you right away!
```

Joe responds to the text as he's directed to.

```
Joe
joe@joesmith.com
```

Shortly thereafter, Joe receives a second and final text message response.

```
Hi Joe, I've gone ahead and sent the
```

slides to your email address, and you should have it there now. By the way, I'll be at the conference through the end of the day tomorrow, and I'd love to connect personally. Come find me in the hallway between sessions!

Joe promptly checks his email, and sure enough finds the slide deck already in his inbox while you are still on stage!

Shortly after the talk, Joe indeed comes to find you in the hallway, has a chat with you and then continues on with the conference.

The next day, Joe is checking his email when he finds another email from you in his inbox, this time telling him a bit more about you and your story (the first of several indoctrination emails that are automatically sent out to new contacts). Having just watched you speak and then subsequently talking with you for a few minutes, Joe's beginning to get a good feel for you.

Upon getting home from the conference, Joe finds another email from you in his inbox that tells him another story that he can relate to. Digging your business card out of his materials, he goes out to your website and opts into one of your e-books to start learning a little bit more. The system promptly delivers the e-book to him, and then tries to set him up to be offered product in the near future. However, because Joe has already opted in several days earlier during your talk at the conference, his information is already in the system. As such, the system is already sitting in a delay, waiting for the appropriate time to send him the marketing sequence for the low barrier offer.

A day later, Joe receives the first of three emails that tell him about your low barrier offer (an individual product marketing funnel), which he decides to purchase after the third email. During the purchase, Joe actually chooses to buy two of the three one-click upsells that are attached to the product as well. He receives his products, and then he continues to receive good, solid, content-based emails (a general delivery sequence) from you for the next three weeks (specified in the delay sequence).

Three weeks after purchasing the low barrier offer, Joe receives another offer from you. Because Joe purchased the low barrier offer and two of the three upsells that were associated with the product, the conveyor belt knows which individual product funnel to place him into and takes the appropriate action. This time, however, Joe is not interested in the product being offered and lets four marketing emails pass by without taking any action. Following the fourth email, he is returned to general delivery for a month of rapport-building.

This entire process continues over and over, with Joe being offered a new product every three to four weeks. Eventually, when Joe has been offered each product that you available, he's brought back to the products that he passed on the first time around.

What's truly genius about this entire process is that you can set this up on such a systemic basis that any time you have a new product, all you have to do is launch the product and add it right into your conveyor belt. In doing so, every client like Joe will automatically be offered that product at the right time. It is a beautiful thing, and it's a fabulous way to 10X your business.

Real Life Example: Marketing Conveyor Belts

One of our clients runs a multimillion dollar business selling resistance bands, and generates hundreds of brand new leads every week via new product sales as well as ongoing social media marketing. After several years of struggling to monetize those weekly leads via web-based exercise programs that tie into the the physical product, he turned to our agency for help.

Within just a few weeks, we were able to completely automate the process of moving a new buyer through an indoctrination and rapport-building process, and developed a marketing conveyor belt for him that was able to effectively monetize his on-demand and live workout products, providing a steady stream of passive income for his company that provides the perfect compliment to his line of resistance bands.

Exercise: Marketing Conveyor Belts

We've just gone through some extremely advanced material, and I really want you to be able to apply it to your business.

Conveyor belts are much easier to understand when you can visually look at them. While there was a small diagram earlier in this chapter that showed an incredibly simplified model of how this works, I'd like to give you the opportunity to take a look at this in a more detailed way.

Once again, I've prepared some PDFs for you that you'll want to download.

Text the word SIMPLE to (231) 222-4118

Follow the instructions. You'll be prompted for your email address, and in just a few short moments you'll receive an email with a link to download two files.

The first file I'll send you is a high level map of a simplified conveyor belt with sample products

The second file is a duplicate of the first, with the exception that the boxes are blank and have plenty of space to write in.

Print both maps out, and look at the products you listed in in their correct ladder of ascension so that you can forecast out how this might work for you. This process will really help you understand how the marketing conveyor belt works, and how it can help you systemize your business.

Chapter 7. Pulling Back The Curtain

"Making money is art and working is art and good business is the best art." - Andy Warhol

While we've just gone through several hypothetical examples of how all of this works, there's nothing quite like the real thing, right?

Folks, if nothing else, I am a very honest, transparent guy. For that reason, I'd like pull the curtain back and show you a real case study - this book, *Beyond the Marketing Funnel*. So let me show you exactly what I'm doing here so that you can see what this would look like in practice.

There are several reasons I wrote *Beyond The Marketing Funnel*. First of all, while there are plenty of books about online marketing, email marketing, and funnel building, I've oddly never seen one that discusses implementing a comprehensive marketing automation system for your business. Business owners and entrepreneurs need, and frankly, deserve this knowledge at their fingertips, and I believe I've done a good job of doing that in a way that's easy to understand and implement.

Secondly, *Beyond The Marketing Funnel* is an excellent tool for my team and me to use with clients and prospects to explain different aspects of what we do. For instance, when I'm talking with somebody that may not completely understand the concept of indoctrination, I could simply send them a copy of this book and have them review chapter three, which delves into the topic with the necessary level of detail.

Finally, *Beyond the Marketing Funnel* serves as an excellent offline and online lead magnet. From an online perspective, I can repurpose singular chapters of the book as free downloads deliverable in exchange for contact information. Alternately, I could offer a free-plus-shipping offer to give the entire book away for free, but offer a string of one-click-upsells on the backend to monetize the effort.

From an offline perspective, this book literally contains three separate SMS lead magnets. I've already given you the first two lead magnets, but you can get them again below:

1. A sample visual map of an individual product marketing funnel, available with a sample

product and upsells, as well as a fill-in-the-blanks template that you can use. Text the word FUNNEL to (231) 222-4118 to get it now!

2. A sample visual map of a simplified marketing conveyor belt, available with a sample product lead magnets, as well as a fill-in-the-blanks template that you can use. Text the word SIMPLE to (231) 222-4118 to get it now!

The third lead magnet is the granular conveyor belt map. Very similar to the simplified map, the granular map goes far deeper and literally lists every single communication, sequence, timing, and conditional logic that happens within the corresponding simplified map. If that's something that interests you, go ahead and text the word GRANULAR to (231) 222-4118 to get it now!

After you opt into any one of my lead magnets, you'll be automatically added to my indoctrination sequence where I'll tell you a little bit more about my story, and how my agency, Rockstar Coding, has made incredible impacts in businesses just like yours.

Finally, Rockstar has a variety of products that I'll share with you as well. An agency that is both an

Infusionsoft Certified Partner as well as a Certified Ontraport Consultant, Rockstar offers a variety of services including a library of prebuilt funnel and automation systems for both Infusionsoft and Ontraport, custom automation mapping and implementation, and authority-generating book publishing.

Exercise: Granular Maps

If you have not yet done so, I highly suggest taking a look at a proper granular conveyor belt map.

Text the word GRANULAR to (231) 222-4118

Follow the instructions. You'll be prompted for your email address, and in just a few short moments.

This is an example of a real map that we use to chart out and build the entirety of a real system from lead magnets to individual product marketing funnels and delays. Study it and see how you can adapt the concepts therein to your business!

Chapter 8. Working With Me

"The way to get started is to quit talking and begin doing." - Walt Disney

Beyond The Marketing Funnel provides an excellent introduction to the concept of marketing automation.

Part one of this book is comprised of chapters one through five, where we cover the individual components of marketing automation in detail. Fundamentally, this begins with the concept of chain reactions and how that can play out within the construct of your marketing.

Then we covered lead intake and the different types of lead magnets, as well as how we can use indoctrination to systematically build rapport with our prospects and clients alike.

We discussed how the ladder of ascension functions, and how it plays into a modern product library. Finally, we covered the two fundamental types of funnels - the product library marketing funnel, and the individual product marketing funnel.

Part two of this book is comprised of chapters six and seven, where we design a much more cohesive system within our marketing automation system, providing both hypothetical and real life examples.

Taking it Further

Marketing automation may well be the single most powerful system that you can implement into your business to propel it forward, and the ideas and concepts in this book will serve you well when executed correctly. With that said, there are still a variety of things that I'm unable to properly cover within the constructs of this book because they are either constantly changing or because they are specific to you and your business. These are places where I can personally help you out.

Tools

While I did take some time to list out a few different marketing automation frameworks, it's a truth that these frameworks are always changing, and there are new ones coming out all the time that do different things. More importantly, different tools are more appropriate for different businesses depending on what you are doing, and your existing situation. Making these types of assessments and recommendations is an area where I can assist you greatly.

KPIs

We haven't touched upon metrics at all in this book, which is the only way to really understand whether or not a specific marketing process is effective. While generalities can be made by the type of business that you're talking about, KPIs (or key performance indicators) are often unique to each business depending on their unique processes and goals. Therefore, it's wise to do some consulting work first to make sure that what we are measuring and looking to improve is inline with our overall growth goals. Again, making these types of assessments and recommendations is an area where I can assist you greatly.

Custom Automation Mapping

Time and time again, potential clients approach me wanting my firm's assistance, but without even a vague understanding of where they want to go or how they want to get there. In this instance, we can jointly put together a custom marketing automation map that describes exactly what the systems should look like so that they can be properly built. I can work with you through a consultative process to identify and prepare a custom marketing automation map on your behalf that any competent marketing automation team can implement and execute.

Implementation

Then, of course, there's setting everything up. I often like to say that nothing is rocket science except rocket science... and even rocket science is pretty easy when you know how to do it. That said, setting up a marketing conveyor belt is a very complicated task and it requires a lot of understanding expertise. My team at Rockstar Coding is incredibly adept and providing these types of implementation services, and can help you build your marketing automation systems with expert care and precision.

Get Started

From experience, I've found that it's fairly common for business owners and entrepreneurs like yourself to be a little unsure about what type of strategies you may need - after all, you are an expert in your field, not necessarily online marketing and marketing automation. Sometimes, a simple funnel or two are in order, while other times a full conveyor belt is really what's required in order to propel your business forward.

Because my passion is in helping business owners and entrepreneurs leverage marketing automation to start, grow, and thrive in their businesses, I've set up a process where you and I can get on the phone together for 20 minutes or so to discuss your business and goals.

I'll share more with you about that in a minute, but first I want you to see what other entrepreneurs just like you have said about working with me:

> "Your business needs better automated marketing and more sales. Nothing else matters. I run several multimillion dollar businesses and a global franchise and Mick's team at Rockstar is invaluable in helping me with web tech and marketing automation so we can do what we do best which is make the sale and service our clients. This guy's character is second to none, and his experience and expertise is invaluable in helping me grow my empire."
>
> *Bedros Keuilian*
> *Author, CEO of Fit Body Boot Camp*

"I've worked with Mick and Rockstar Coding for two years now. Mick has a gift for seeing the bigger picture in business. He's helped me maximize my ability to help my customers and my bottom line. The mistake that many info marketers make, including me, is that the focus is strictly on the front end of the business with no real purpose or plan for follow up and profits. Mick has solved this for me by helping me build an entire back end of my business. Mick's vision has allowed me to integrate all my offerings in a systematized and automated way. I'd venture to say that my business is no longer just a 'promotion' business but a real business with more predictable income. In addition to building this system for me, Mick and his team are easy to work, accountable and affordable. My only regret about working with Mick is that I wish I started working with him sooner. Thank you for everything Mick, I can't give anyone a higher recommendation to work with you."

Shawna Kaminski
Owner, MyBikiniBelly.com / ShawnaK.com

"Over the 12 years I've had my marketing firm, I've had the opportunity to work with some amazing mentors. I've also gotten to work with several very high-powered funnel development companies, including Sixth Division and some of the top leaders in the industry.

Hands down, the most effective and supportive mentor I have worked with around funnel development has been Mick Olinik. Mick has taken so much time and shared so much of his expertise to help my company become more successful. We have literally tripled our revenue working with him.

He also helped us put systems in place and develop procedures so that we were able to handle the massive influx of clients that his funnel created. And he helped me create a product leading to passive revenue streams, so I could support my community 24/7.

This is one of the most effective people I have ever collaborated with, and I am grateful to know him. I can't recommend Mick highly enough as a mentor and a funnel development expert.

Finally, Mick's also been a guest and spoken on my stage and support my community, and that was an amazing experience. He got the highest scores and was voted best speaker at both conferences. We intend to have him back over and over."

Mary Agnes Antonopoulos
CMO of Viral Integrity Marketing

"I met Mick at a Mastermind and waited for 3 months until his schedule opened up to work with me. I've spent a sickening amount of money with business developers and web developers in the past, I cannot even tell you. Mick worked hard and brought the right team around me so that quickly, and affordably, I was finally ready to help people. He has a personality that you'll never get sick of. You'd be stupid not to hire this guy."

Dr. Mary Clifton
Owner, Dr. Mary's Reset Revolution

"Before working with Mick, I was confused and feeling bottlenecked with the migration of my sales page site so that I could make simple changes on my own. Mick took the time to explain my options. Mick's endless patience and heartfelt advice allowed us to move beyond the obstacles holding us back. Now we can focus on moving our business forward in order to help more people and achieve the lifestyle we desire."

Amy Lewis
Owner, BanishYourBellyBloat.com

I really am passionate about helping business owners and entrepreneurs build their businesses in the right direction, and regardless of whether I'm the right person to provide services to you, there's no doubt in my mind that my experience and advice can help steer *you* in the right direction, too.

If I don't think I can personally help you quickly grow your business, income, and impact, then I'll let you know and I'll tell you who can. But if I can help you, then I'll let you know what steps I think you should take, and whether or not it makes sense for use to work together.

Fair enough?

To book your free call with me, visit
rockstarcoding.com/advice
or
Text the word ADVICE to (231) 222-4118

Somebody from my team will connect with you to coordinate our 20 minute call.

Looking forward to helping you reach the next level!

Mick Olinik

About The Author

MICK OLINIK is an online marketing expert and business model guru who's been working with the Web since the mid 1990s. As such, Mick's had the luxury of having a front row seat to the technical development and sociological trends of online marketing and sales from their very beginnings, bringing a rare depth of experience and expertise to his clients. A serial entrepreneur and the CEO of Rockstar Enterprises, Mick's passion is in helping entrepreneurs and business owners expand their reach and help more people by leveraging marketing automation to start, grow and thrive in their businesses.

Find out more at www.Amazon.com/author/MickOlinik

Or visit www.MickOlinik.com

Other Books By Mick Olinik

The WordPress Anthology: Get Under The Hood Of WordPress!

The Modern Day Printing Press: An Unofficial Guide to WordPress for Small Business

Can I Ask You For A Favor?

If you enjoyed this book, found it useful, or otherwise then I'd really appreciate it if you would post a short review on Amazon. I do read all the reviews personally so that I can continually write what people are wanting.

If you'd like to leave a review then please visit the link below:

http://amzn.to/2oSPHBA

Thanks for your support!

Made in United States
Troutdale, OR
11/03/2026

56852541R00069